Pray Through The Pain

Weekly Prayer Journal

By Charlise R. Walker

Biblical Scriptures are from the New International Version (NIV) and King James Version (KJV). The Holy Bible

Cover design and created from the Canva Pro version by Frans Van Heerden.

Find other books under the pen name Charlise R. Rice

Books & Merch website https://www.CharliseRice.com
Professional Resource Consultant website https://www.LisesBusiness.com

Printed in the United States of America ISBN 979-8-9879207-0-1

Pray Through The Pain

I started writing to express my feelings or hide my feelings on paper. As I grew older, I learned in one of my undergrad psychology classes, that writing is a good way to cope. For myself, writing helps me process and regulate my emotions.

Journaling will allow you to release emotions, and write your heart's desires, questions, and concerns while pondering on the words of God. This will also help you to focus and build a relationship with Him. With these scriptures, lean on the promises of God. Seek Him first and pray through your pain of emotions.

My prayer for you is that whatever you are praying for in your journal that God brings the rain to shower you with blessings of comfort, survival, healing, and freedom, whatever your journey is, your harvest is coming.

Don't give up, God loves you.

- If you or you know someone that is suicidal, please call or text 988 for help.
- If you are in a domestic violent relationship, please call 1.800.799.SAFE (7233) or Text "START" to 88788 for help.

Prayer Poem

Enter my body, Lord
And cleanse me out
Give me knowledge, so I know
What you're all about
Wrap me with your
Presence Lord
And keep me safe
Take over my mind
Fill me
Cleanse me
Wrap me
Help me
Work me
Accept me
Love me
Understand me
Release me
Comfort me
Peace be with me
Reject the enemy
God I continually seek thee

From my book, Take Pain and Walk: Collection of Poems

Week 1

I will lift up mine eyes unto the hills, from whence cometh my help. My help cometh from the Lord, which made heaven and earth.

Psalms 121:1-2 (KJV)

Help doesn't come from the hills, it comes from the creator. No one is exempt from trials, or tribulations. Things happen, situations come up against us, and problems trying to overcome. Most things are beyond our own control. One thing is for sure, if you need help, ask for it, and pray for it. If the only thing you can utter from your mouth is "help me" then so be it. You may need help with healing, frustration, difficulty, anxiety, disappointments, doubt, anger, stress, worries, and/or fear. Whatever is troubling you this week or from the past, write it down, pray, and ask God to help you. God's power supersedes.

_____

_____

_____

_____

_____

_____

Week 2

Trust in the LORD with all your heart and lean not on your own understanding;

Proverbs 3:5 (NIV)

There were a lot of situations I went through that I didn't understand. I questioned myself, why was it happening to me? But I've learned and disciplined myself to go to God. I say, God wherever you want me to be, I am there. I look at the greater good which is getting to the light at the end of the tunnel. I know this situation will change, I have to hold on and let God. Trust in the Lord and His strength to get you through.

_____

_____

_____

_____

_____

_____

_____

_____

Week 3

Let us not become weary in doing good, for at the proper time we will reap a harvest if we do not give up.

Galations 6:9 (NIV)

Don't get tired of doing the right thing. Doing the right thing can be tough depending on the circumstance. We reap what we sow. Continue to do the good, be the good, and good will come back to you. Bring all your concerns to Him and reflect on the good you have done.

_____

_____

_____

_____

_____

_____

_____

_____

_____

Week 4

Finally, be strong in the Lord and in his mighty power. Put on the full armor of God, so that you can take your stand against the devil's schemes. For our struggle is not against flesh and blood, but against the rulers, against the authorities, against the powers of this dark world and against the spiritual forces of evil in the heavenly realms. Therefore put on the full armor of God, so that when the day of evil comes, you may be able to stand your ground, and after you have done everything, to stand.

Ephesians 6:10–13 (NIV)

Sometimes in life, it feels like we can't get ahead and everything we have is under attack. These verses remind us to protect ourselves and our minds. When evil comes against you, stand up with God. Put on the full armor of God, and He will help you fight. Continue reading the verses in this chapter in your bible about the armor of God. What is trying to hinder you?

_____

_____

_____

_____

_____

_____

_____

_____

Week 5

What, then, shall we say in response to these things? If God is for us, who can be against us?

Romans 8:31 (NIV)

Remember that "God is for us" and be confident in the face of opposition. God is almighty and powerful. We may suffer, but we will not be destroyed, no matter how bad things seem. What opposition is trying to come up against you?

_____

_____

_____

_____

_____

_____

_____

_____

_____

Week 6

Clap your hands, all you nations;
shout to God with cries of joy.

Psalms 47:1 (NIV)

Praise be to God! Put on some gospel praise music. Be thankful, be grateful, and praise your way through this. Some days you may not want to but do it anyway and give God the GLORY. Clap your hands and shout out to HIM. Hallelujah is the highest praise! Hey, you may want to clap to your own song. What did you praise Him for this week?

_____

_____

_____

_____

_____

_____

_____

_____

_____

Week 7

*He will cover you with his feathers,
and under his wings you will find refuge;
his faithfulness will be your shield and
rampart.*

Psalms 91:4 (NIV)

I had a vivid dream once that God had my son and me in his hands way above the clouds, carrying us over the city. From then on, I know God will take care of us and has us covered. God is covering you. He is our comfort zone and our safety net. How can He be your shield and rampart?

_____

_____

_____

_____

_____

_____

_____

_____

_____

Week 8

Now faith is confidence in what we hope for and assurance about what we do not see.

Hebrews 11:1 (NIV)

There have been plenty of times when I did not know how but I knew I would get through my circumstances. Faith in God is not seeing when you are in the tunnel but knowing you will get through it. His word also says that if you have faith the size of a mustard seed, nothing will be impossible! What do you need faith for this week?

_____

_____

_____

_____

_____

_____

_____

_____

Week 9

Have I not commanded you? Be strong and courageous. Do not be afraid; do not be discouraged, for the Lord your God will be with you wherever you go."

Joshua 1:9 (NIV)

This is one of my favorite scriptures! I moved to Texas without having ever been here until the day I moved here. Though I know God lined everything up for me, I was scared. I didn't have a job and didn't know anyone. I knew I had to do better for myself and my son. I wanted better, and everything led to Texas. God is omnipresent, meaning he is everywhere present, and his holy spirit guides us. How are you being strong and courageous this week?

_____

_____

_____

_____

_____

_____

_____

_____

Week 10

As the rain and the snow
come down from heaven,
and do not return to it
without watering the earth
and making it bud and flourish,
so that it yields seed for the sower and
bread for the eater,
so is my word that goes out from my
mouth:
It will not return to me empty,
but will accomplish what I desire
and achieve the purpose for which I sent
it.

Isaiah 55:10-11 (NIV)

God's word never comes back void. He is the truth and the light. His word gives us life, hope, and comfort. Continue to use his word and read it. This will help you grow spiritually. Keep leaning on his word and promises. Thank God for his word and his promises.

_____

_____

_____

_____

_____

_____

_____

_____

_____

Week 11

For our light affliction, which is but for a moment, worketh for us a far more exceeding and eternal weight of glory; While we look not at the things which are seen, but at the things which are not seen: for the things which are seen are temporal; but the things which are not seen are eternal.

2 Corinthians 4:17-18 (KJV)

It is not easy when you are suffering, in pain, or distress. You don't have to do it alone. Go to God with your troubles. With God, any suffering in this life is outweighed by what is to come. Hold on, don't give up when it seems unbearable. Instead, put the weight on Him and give it to God. Tell Him what's been troubling you.

_____

_____

_____

_____

_____

_____

_____

_____

_____

Week 12

Therefore confess your sins to each other and pray for each other so that you may be healed. The prayer of a righteous person is powerful and effective.

James 5:16 (NIV)

Admittedly confess your faults freely to someone you may have done wrong. It is ok to seek forgiveness if you are able. Confessing and asking for forgiveness is for yourself. This allows you to release nagging feelings and be free in your mind. We are to confess our sins to God as He is faithful, forgives us, and cleanses us from all unrighteousness. We are also to pray for others willingly.

_____

_____

_____

_____

_____

_____

_____

_____

Week 13

*No temptation has overtaken you
except what is common to mankind.
And God is faithful; he will not let you
be tempted beyond what you can bear.
But when you are tempted, he will also
provide a way out so that you can
endure it.*

1 Corinthians 10:13 (NIV)

I have been tempted to go back to something I know was wrong in the first place. Going back to trying old ways that didn't work then and sure it will not work now. We get tempted without patience at times. We may feel the process should work faster, or I am good if I do this one more time. If you get caught up in temptation, God is the way out and will make a way out. What a testimony it will be! What temptation do you need to be free of?

_____

_____

_____

_____

_____

_____

_____

Week 14

I cried out to God for help; I cried out to God to hear me. When I was in distress, I sought the Lord; at night I stretched out untiring hands and my soul refused to be comforted. You kept my eyes from closing; I was too troubled to speak. "Will the Lord reject forever?

Psalms 77:1 - 7 (NIV)

I remember being so tired of my situation that all I could do was cry—disappointment, rejection after rejection. I was too tired to keep trying and wondered if God had heard me. I kept questioning how long I must wait. God hears your prayers and will answer in due time. I charge you to read the entire book of Psalms 77. Continue to Pray because He hears you.

_____

_____

_____

_____

_____

_____

_____

_____

Week 15

This is the confidence we have in approaching God: that if we ask anything according to his will, he hears us.

1 John 5:14 (NIV)

Tell God your hopes, your dreams, your heart's troubles. Tell him what is on your mind. Continue to pray while waiting and ask him. He wants to hear from you, and he is waiting. What is it you need to approach God with this week?

_____

_____

_____

_____

_____

_____

_____

_____

_____

Week 16

"So do not worry, saying, 'What shall we eat?' or 'What shall we drink?' or "What shall we wear?' For the pagans run after all these things, and your heavenly Father knows that you need them. But seek first His kingdom and His righteousness, and all these things will be given to you as well. Therefore do not worry about tomorrow, for tomorrow will worry about itself. Each day has enough trouble of its own."

Matthew 6:31-34 (NIV)

Rely on God rather than ourselves. We can't do it all. I tried to but learned that I needed help. Go to Him for comfort, strength, and reassurance, acknowledging who He is and what He can do. So do what you can control today. God provides everything we need. Seek God first; he will reveal your needs and provide your necessities. What is troubling you this week?

_____

_____

_____

_____

_____

_____

_____

_____

Even so faith, if it hath not works, is dead, being alone. Yea, a man may say, Thou hast faith, and I have works: shew me thy faith without thy works, and I will shew thee my faith by my works.

James 2:17-18 (KJV)

Another one of my favorite scriptures. I believe this scripture is saying don't just sit there. You have faith now; show your faith with your works! It is good to believe and have faith that you can pass a test but still study. Do the work. Do the work God called you to do as well.

_____

_____

_____

_____

_____

_____

_____

_____

_____

Week 18

But my God shall supply all your need according to his riches in glory by Christ Jesus.

Philipians 4:19 (KJV)

Paul wrote this in gratitude and as a reminder that God will supply all you need. When I moved to Texas, though, I didn't have all the resources, everything lined up, and all was provided for my son and me to move. Gas, food, money, etc. At the time, I didn't have a job. Yet I am very thankful for the process, it wasn't easy, but still, I stand. Thank God for the process as it is part of your journey.

_____

_____

_____

_____

_____

_____

_____

_____

Week 19

Now to him who is able to do immeasurably more than all we ask or imagine, according to his power that is at work within us

Ephesians 3:20 (NIV)

God is able to do abundantly beyond our greatest prayers, hopes, or dreams. When I look at my life now, I am at peace, safe, and confident. He is a way-maker. Not in my wildest dreams have I ever thought about moving to Texas; he made a way out! What do you need God to do this week?

_____

_____

_____

_____

_____

_____

_____

_____

Week 20

Looking unto Jesus the author and finisher of our faith; who for the joy that was set before him endured the cross, despising the shame, and is set down at the right hand of the throne of God.

Hebrews 12:2 (KJV)

The Bible is a love story. Jesus gave his life so that we could live. Agape love is the highest form of love. Jesus bore a lot of pain and shame yet traded his life. Now that is love.

_____

_____

_____

_____

_____

_____

_____

_____

_____

_____

Week 21

Dearly beloved, avenge not yourselves, but rather give place unto wrath: for it is written, Vengeance is mine; I will repay, saith the Lord.

Romans 12:19 (KJV)

I wanted my son's biological father and ex-husband to suffer from the physical and mental abuse they put me through. I used to wish I had an older brother to handle them in the wrong way. But God's word says vengeance is HIS. Plus, God's wrath can be worse than what I could do. However, as a Christian, I've gotten to a place of peace and pray they get right with God, even if I never receive a formal apology. We don't need to retaliate because the Lord will avenge for us. What do you need Him to handle for you?

_____

_____

_____

_____

_____

_____

Week 22

Do nothing out of selfish ambition or vain conceit. Rather, in humility value others above yourselves, not looking to your own interests but each of you to the interests of the others.

Philippians 2:3–4 (NIV)

This week's verse relates to how we display our behavior to people. How do we treat people, display love, be humble, and be patient? Are we looking out for others only to gain something for ourselves? If you value yourself, it will show in how you treat people. I charge you to read the entire chapter because it speaks of unity, love, and humility. Surround yourself with the right people and you will get the same in return.

_____

_____

_____

_____

_____

_____

_____

"Have faith in God," Jesus answered. "Truly I tell you, if anyone says to this mountain, 'Go, throw yourself into the sea,' and does not doubt in their heart but believes that what they say will happen, it will be done for them. Therefore I tell you, whatever you ask for in prayer, believe that you have received it, and it will be yours. And when you stand praying, if you hold anything against anyone, forgive them, so that your Father in heaven may forgive you your sins."

Mark 11:22-25 (NIV)

These are some of my husband's go-to verses during tough times. Imagine the mountains are your troubles, circumstances, pain, situations, temptation, whatever it may be; Jesus came so that we have life. Jesus said these words. We must believe and ask in prayer to move these obstacles, mountains, valleys, and bumps in the road so we can proceed with life and tell a great testimony. Do this so you can have peace in your mind and heart. What mountain do you need Him to move to this week?

_____

_____

_____

_____

_____

_____

_____

Week 24

Make a joyful noise unto the LORD, all ye lands. Serve the LORD with gladness: Come before his presence with singing.

Psalms 100:1-2 (KJV)

Psalms 100 is one of my son's favorite verses. My son definitely loves some good gospel and praise music. This verse is a Psalm of praise. Singing is one way to praise and worship God. I learned that worship is emptying yourself to God. Don't focus on what you need Him to do but worship Him for who He is. Ask God to fill you up after you empty yourself to Him. He can fill you with visions, hope, love, grace, etc.

_____

_____

_____

_____

_____

_____

_____

_____

Week 25

*So do not fear, for I am with you;
do not be dismayed, for I am your
God. I will strengthen you and help
you; I will uphold you with my
righteous right hand.*

Isaiah 41:10 (NIV)

I admit I have allowed fear and doubt to enter my mind and hinder me from moving forward on some things. I paused a long time before writing this prayer journal for you because I doubted I was good enough. The holy spirit kept pressing me to do this, and I am good enough. Don't let fear and doubt stop you or get you off your path completely. God has your back! Tell Him your fears so that he can help and strengthen you.

_____

_____

_____

_____

_____

_____

_____

Week 26

For I am the Lord your God
who takes hold of your right hand
and says to you, Do not fear;
I will help you.

Isaiah 41:13 (NIV)

When I left Michigan to move to Texas, God lined everything up. No way I did it all by myself. When you move forward, our Father in heaven is seemingly saying, take his hand, let him guide you. Take His hand by telling Him what has been troubling you this week.

_____

_____

_____

_____

_____

_____

_____

_____

_____

Week 27

Those who sow with tears
will reap with songs of joy.
Those who go out weeping,
carrying seed to sow,
will return with songs of joy,
carrying sheaves with them.

Psalms 126:5-6 (NIV)

Count it all, JOY! Your tear drops are planting seeds. God sees your tears. You may sow tears of sadness, but you will reap joy soon. Praise be to GOD! Tell God why you are hurting or sad and crying.

_____

_____

_____

_____

_____

_____

_____

_____

_____

_____

Week 28

Humble yourselves, therefore, under God's mighty hand, that he may lift you up in due time. Cast all your anxiety on him because he cares for you.

1 Peter 5:6–7 (NIV)

Tell God all about your worries, problems, issues, nervousness, and uncertainties. This can be weighing heavily on your mind. You will be able to withhold because God will bring you up in his timing. Release what is troubling you.

_____

_____

_____

_____

_____

_____

_____

_____

_____

_____

Week 29

"Come to me, all you who
are weary and burdened,
and I will give you rest.
Take my yoke upon you
and learn from me, for I
am gentle and humble in
heart, and you will find rest
for your souls.
For my yoke is easy and my
burden is light."

Matthew 11:28-30 (NIV)

Life can get hard and makes our souls weary. It doesn't get easier as a Christian, but your faith grows stronger. God is inviting us to give him your yoke for his, and you will find rest in your weary soul. What do you need to give God this week to lighten your burdens?

_____

_____

_____

_____

_____

_____

_____

_____

_____

Week 30

We are hard pressed on every side,
but not crushed; perplexed, but not
in despair; persecuted, but not
abandoned; struck down, but not
destroyed. We always carry around
in our body the death of Jesus, so
that the life of Jesus may also be
revealed in our body.

2 Corinthians 4:8-10 (NIV)

Life can throw us around hard! Think of everything you have been through, and you made it out just fine. We were built to last! Our circumstances can perplex us, but God saved us, and He will sustain us. What is troubling you this week?

_____

_____

_____

_____

_____

_____

_____

_____

_____

The Lord is my light and my salvation; whom shall I fear? the Lord is the strength of my life; of whom shall I be afraid?

Psalms 27:1 (KJV)

This scripture is total trust and guidance in God. David wrote this passage to exemplify that he knew he would be rescued from his circumstances and have complete confidence in God's will. Lord keeps us safe, and we have no reason to fear. In total confidence, write what you believe God will rescue you from.

_____

_____

_____

_____

_____

_____

_____

_____

_____

Week 32

The LORD himself goes before you and will be with you; he will never leave you nor forsake you. Do not be afraid; do not be discouraged."

Dueteronomy 31:8 (NIV)

Don't be afraid, and don't be discouraged. I came to Texas, where I had never been and never met anyone, barely knowing my cousin. God was already there, here, everywhere. We may not see the path but have faith in where you are headed because he has already made a way. His word always prevails. What do you need Him for this week?

_____

_____

_____

_____

_____

_____

_____

_____

Week 33

Through Jesus, therefore, let us
continually offer to God a sacrifice
of praise—the fruit of lips that
openly profess his name.

Hebrews 13:15 (NIV)

Praise His Holy name! Praise him for what you have been through or going through. No way I could have made it out of abusive relationships without God. He was the one that covered my son and me. I would not have made it to Texas without his direction. So let us continually thank Him for giving us another day!

_____

_____

_____

_____

_____

_____

_____

_____

_____

But he said to me, "My grace is sufficient for you, for my power is made perfect in weakness." Therefore I will boast all the more gladly about my weaknesses, so that Christ's power may rest on me. That is why, for Christ's sake, I delight in weaknesses, in insults, in hardships, in persecutions, in difficulties. For when I am weak, then I am strong.

2 Corinthians 12:9–10 (NIV)

When we are weak, we are strong. Only the power of Jesus Christ works this way in our weakness. Continue to stand on His promises. He knows that by allowing us to experience failure, hardships, pain, and struggle, we will grow stronger in our faith and become closer to Him. Ask Him to continue to strengthen you.

_____

_____

_____

_____

_____

_____

_____

_____

_____

Week 35

Why, my soul, are you downcast?
Why so disturbed within me? Put your
hope in God, for I will yet praise him,
my Savior and my God.

Psalms 42:11 (NIV)

Sometimes you have to encourage yourself. When we focus too long on our frustrations, and circumstances, it will take away our peace in the present moment. Pull yourself out of a dark place, get control of your thoughts and mind by reminding yourself of the promises of God and putting your hope in Him.

_____

_____

_____

_____

_____

_____

_____

_____

_____

Week 36

Let the peace of Christ rule in
your hearts, since as members of
one body you were called to peace.
And be thankful.

Colossians 3:15 (NIV)

God doesn't promise us a life free of pain or hardship, but he does provide the strength to endure. We have to face our pain and difficulties, not run away from them. We can do this by declaring that Jesus Christ is in charge. If you're frightened, tell him. If you're scared, run to him. If you're weak, ask for help. Ask God to help you.

_____

_____

_____

_____

_____

_____

_____

_____

Week 37

When pride comes, then comes
disgrace, but with humility comes
wisdom. Let the peace of Christ rule
in your hearts, since as members of
one body you were called to peace.
And be thankful.

Proverbs 11:2 (NIV)

Don't think that you can do everything all by yourself. This is one way to get tired very quickly! At one point, I thought I didn't need anyone's help, and I'd rather do it myself. The worst thing you can have is pride. Pride distorts decision-making ability. Humility will lift you before God. Ask God for help or have the courage to ask others for help when you need it.

_____

_____

_____

_____

_____

_____

_____

_____

Week 38

For we live by faith, not by sight.

2 Corinthians 5:7 (NIV)

A simple verse, but yet sometimes hard to do. What we see and feel, such as suffering, financial challenges, fear, anger, anxiety, confusion, unhappiness, hurt, whatever it is, may be hard to focus on your faith. I challenge you to have faith as the bible instructs many times. Walking by faith means making it a habit to live this way every time circumstances arise. Count the unseen things as you put your trust and faith in Jesus Christ our Lord and Savior.

_____

_____

_____

_____

_____

_____

_____

Week 39

For we do not have a high priest who is unable to empathize with our weaknesses, but we have one who has been tempted in every way, just as we are—yet he did not sin. Let us then approach God's throne of grace with confidence, so that we may receive mercy and find grace to help us in our time of need.

Hebrews 4:15-16 (NIV)

If you ever read about all the things Jesus went through from the time he was in the womb of Mary until his death on the cross, you know he can understand your circumstances too. He can sympathize with our weaknesses. You can approach Him boldly and let your request be known to him because he knows. What do you need to tell Him this week?

_____

_____

_____

_____

_____

_____

_____

_____

Week 40

Rejoice always, pray continually, give thanks in all circumstances; for this is God's will for you in Christ Jesus.

1 Thessalonians 5:16–18 (NIV)

This is God's will for you as a Christian. He wants to hear from us. It will strengthen you. I know it will be hard to rejoice or give thanks if you just found out you have been diagnosed with an incurable disease. Try it this way. Be thankful that the doctors found it. Praise God that maybe doctors can begin the process of healing. So pray through the process that God heals your pain and allow His will to be done.

_____

_____

_____

_____

_____

_____

_____

_____

Week 41

The thief cometh not, but for to steal, and to kill, and to destroy: I am come that they might have life, and that they might have it more abundantly.

John 10:10 (KJV)

Jesus said this scripture in context to false spiritual teachers. However, when given the opportunity, the devil can do the same. Think about Job in the bible. The devil will attack your weaknesses, try to weaken your mind and what/whom you care about the most, and dampen your mood. Jesus Christ came so we can live in abundance in joy, love, happiness, and peace. Go to Him to experience abundant life.

_____

_____

_____

_____

_____

_____

_____

_____

Week 42

A good man brings good things out of the good stored up in his heart, and an evil man brings evil things out of the evil stored up in his heart. For the mouth speaks what the heart is full of.

Luke 6:45 (NIV)

I played basketball for fun, in middle school and high school. I was the Captain of my high school varsity team. I remember saying I wanted to be in the WNBA. I started seeing other women play better than me, I THOUGHT. I stopped playing, and conditioning on my own because I thought I wasn't good enough. When untrue words are spoken, they undervalue who you are. You may say one thing, but the truth in your heart is another. This can lead to anxiety, confusion, fear, and unnecessary worry. These were self-deprecating thoughts I had. If you have self-deprecating thoughts, encourage yourself with the promises of God. Replace those negative thoughts with positive affirmations.

_____

_____

_____

_____

_____

_____

Week 43

*For I know the plans I have for you,"
declares the LORD, "plans to prosper
you and not to harm you, plans to give
you hope and a future.*

Jeremiah 29:11 (NIV)

This verse is one of God's promises and a reminder that he is in control. Though we face difficult situations or circumstances, his plan is always to give us hope and a future. Your situation may not make sense now as you are going through a storm, but God's plan is still good.

_____

_____

_____

_____

_____

_____

_____

_____

_____

He that dwelleth in the secret place of the most High shall abide under the shadow of the Almighty. I will say of the LORD, He is my refuge and my fortress: My God; in him will I trust.

Psalm 91:1-2 (KJV)

I've been in relationships that didn't feel right or comfortable. One of which I was not because I was in a physically abusive relationship. Though I fought back, I did not feel comfortable or safe. God is a constant, trusted companion. He will protect you protection amid hardship and danger. Focus on trusting and being loyal to God.

_____

_____

_____

_____

_____

_____

_____

_____

_____

Week 45

if this is so, then the Lord knows how to rescue the godly from trials and to hold the unrighteous for punishment on the day of judgment.

2 Peter 2:9 (NIV)

It may seem like people have done you wrong by being deceitful, using you, or lying, and they are not held accountable for their actions. God always has the final judgment. His purposes and plan will prevail so we are not overcome by evil. Even when we fail or are going through difficult times. No matter how terrible things become, we have an assurance that God's judgment of evil will surely happen.

_____

_____

_____

_____

_____

_____

_____

Week 46

I have told you these things, so that in me you may have peace. In this world you will have trouble. But take heart! I have overcome the world."

John 16:33 (NIV)

Jesus wants you to experience an abundance of peace and safety. Though we are not exempt from pain, suffering, trials, and tribulation, Jesus left the Holy Spirit to comfort us. What is it that you need to tell Him so that you can have peace?

_____

_____

_____

_____

_____

_____

_____

_____

_____

Week 47

but those who hope in the Lord
will renew their strength.
They will soar on wings like eagles;
they will run and not grow weary,
they will walk and not be faint.

Isaiah 40:31 (NIV)

Life's circumstances can really wear you down and out. Hard circumstances can break us in spirit too. It can also leave us wondering and questioning where is God or does he care. This scripture is one of God's promises of care and strength for the weary. I encourage you to hang in there because GOD will renew your strength. What do you need from Him this week?

_____

_____

_____

_____

_____

_____

_____

_____

Week 48

Taste and see that the Lord is good;
blessed is the one who takes
refuge in him.

Psalm 34:8 (NIV)

I love to read the book of Psalms because there are good poetry, songs, and prophetic messages. This Psalm verse invites us to experience the Lord's goodness. I think about all the things God has brought me out of. Not only bad things but also his goodness in giving me another day and the ability to bless someone else with my knowledge or through our nonprofit. I am truly grateful! How has God been good to you?

_____

_____

_____

_____

_____

_____

_____

Do not be anxious about anything,
but in every situation, by prayer
and petition, with thanksgiving,
present your requests to God.
And the peace of God, which
transcends all understanding, will
guard your hearts and your minds
in Christ Jesus.

Philippians 4:6-7 (NIV)

Prayer is about building a relationship, trusting in God, and seeking his guidance. Leaning on Him in bad times and in good times. His words state that when we are feeling anxious, come to him with our anxieties, and he will give us peace. Continue to pray as it creates discipline and peace and will protect your heart and your mind. What are you feeling anxious about?

_____

_____

_____

_____

_____

_____

_____

_____

Week 50

And we know that in all things God works for the good of those who love him, who have been called according to his purpose.

Romans 8:28 (NIV)

I believe God has a purpose to bring out in every situation or circumstance in our lives. I used to ask God, why am I going through this? As I started to write and pray, I now ask what is your purpose. Ask God to reveal the purpose of His plan during your situation or circumstance.

_____

_____

_____

_____

_____

_____

_____

_____

_____

Week 51

He says, "Be still, and
know that I am God;
I will be exalted
among the nations,
I will be exalted in
the earth.

Psalms 46:10 (NIV)

Everything happens for a reason. God doesn't make any mistakes. We live in a world with many distractions, rushing to do things, frustrations, and short-tempered people. God wants your attention. God is above everything. God is above all our problems. So spend some quiet moments with God and give Him your full attention.

_____

_____

_____

_____

_____

_____

_____

_____

Week 52

Ye are of God, little children, and have overcome them: because greater is he that is in you, than he that is in the world.

1 John 4:4 (KJV)

The Holy Spirit dwells in us. Jesus left us this gift when he died on the cross. The Holy Spirit is what some call our "first mind". That's that nudge that is pressing in your mind to tell you to do something or go right instead of left. That's HIS guidance. Listen to that voice that is telling you to do the right thing. We overcome evil principalities because greater is HE Who is in you than he who is in the world. Continue to pray, believe, and have faith.

_____

_____

_____

_____

_____

_____

_____

I pray that this journal was a blessing to you. I intentionally added more journal pages. You may want to come back and read what you wrote weeks or a year from now to see how you overcame your troubles with God. Share your testimony with someone else so that it may encourage them to put their trust in Him.

As a bonus, here are some YouTube Videos from me to encourage you. Scan the QR Code to get access to these videos.

About the Author

Charlise was born and raised on the eastside of Detroit, Michigan. She loves to write. Writing is a way to release built-up emotions with poetry, talking about her testimony, or helping someone with her professional knowledge.

Charlise currently lives with her family in the north Dallas, TX area. She is a Human Resources Specialist, Professional Resource Specialist, and has earned her Master's degree in Management in Nonprofit Leadership. She is passionate about helping people have the necessary skills to be prepared for the job market and overcome job preparation barriers. She provides services, encourages, and offers educational advice with her business, Lise's Business Enterprise. With Charlise Rice Books and Merch, this allows her to share her creative side with self-published books, designs, and handmade jewelry collections.

Charlise is enlightened to share her experiences and testimonies as well as having the ability to help the community. Charlise has a down-to-earth personality and is not ashamed to tell where her story began. Additional books under Pen names Charlise Rice and Charlise Walker.